T0149577

THE TRUTH ABOUT YOUR BUSINESS

THE TRUTH ABOUT YOUR BUSINESS

**SEVENTY-THREE FOCUS SESSIONS
TO GROW YOUR BUSINESS**

*To find out what your truth is,
start by asking a lot of questions.*

TMIMA GRINVALD

THE TRUTH ABOUT YOUR BUSINESS
Seventy-Three Focus Sessions to Grow Your Business

iUniverse books may be ordered through booksellers or by contacting:

iUniverse
1663 Liberty Drive
Bloomington, IN 47403
www.iuniverse.com
1-800-Authors (1-800-288-4677)

ISBN: 978-1-5320-1302-7 (sc)
ISBN: 978-1-5320-1303-4 (e)

Print information available on the last page.

iUniverse rev. date: 12/16/2016

To my mom and dad. I grew up to believe in myself because you, beyond anyone else, showed me that everything is possible if I put myself 100 percent in the game. With you two gone, your legacy continues with the work I do to coach others to bring their best into this world.

ACKNOWLEDGMENTS

———

I am deeply thankful for my family: my dear husband, Eliyahu Grinvald; my son, Nimrod; and my daughter, Zohar. I have the good fortune to have a loving family who challenge my ideas and support my actions. At times, during Friday night dinners, we share our business-related experiences. While I listen to their stories, I get to formulate stronger viewpoints and build broader references to our world.

I would like to make a special note to my sister, Hanita Ruttner, who kept encouraging me on my journey as a businesswoman, wife, mother, and author.

I would also like to acknowledge my niece, Inbar Ruttner, who help me collate and categorize my blog material as I started on the journey of writing this book.

INTRODUCTION

This book sheds light on different aspects of running your own business. Each session is designed to bring clarity to a specific business area. Sometimes it is not about the knowledge you have in a specific zone; rather, it is about the mind-set you have. Through each concise session, you will uncover an insight unique to you. The questions in each session will help you to focus on getting the most out of that particular area.

I aim to help you see through your own experiences and results to determine what works and what doesn't—what will hold true in the future for your business and what should be left behind in the dust. As a business coach, I ask a lot of questions to help bring clarity to my clients. With that clarity, they can see the truth and become stronger leaders.

The key to getting the most from this book is to begin each session with a clear head. You may want to read one session a day or one session a week. Make sure to take some time to reflect on one before you move on to the next. That will allow you to take your time and honestly answer the questions I present to you, so you can figure out your own truth and start to apply what you have learned.

This book is not about knowing more stuff. It is about applying insights that will help you improve your business.

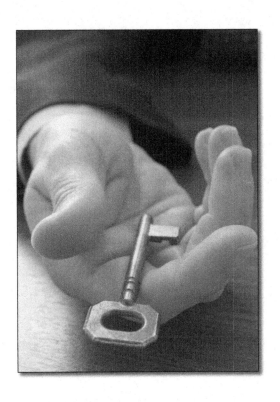

PART 1

IMPLEMENTING AND EVALUATING YOUR STRATEGY

Just as a ship without a navigational chart and with no planned destination will get lost at sea, a business without a strategy will produce unpredictable results. By definition, *strategy* is a careful plan or method for achieving a particular goal, usually over a long period of time. Every successful business has a strategy that aligns actions with the owner's vision. You also need an overall strategy to be able to navigate successfully within a changing economy.

Session 1

DO YOU HAVE NO TIME FOR SETTING A STRATEGY?

Have you ever heard of a CEO informing his board of directors that he has no time for strategy? What if he actually did that? I assume he'd get fired.

Yet business owners let strategy fall off their busy schedules all the time without giving it a second thought. To be sure, you have a lot on your plate. You juggle so many things, and it's only a matter of time until something is dropped. If I asked you why you juggle so many things, you'd probably say that all these activities are urgent. No one would argue.

Strategy is just one of those things you'll get to when you have time—and you never have time.

When did you last make a serious effort to reflect on the strategy you have chosen to lead your business, your career, or your life? How about high-level objectives and a method of addressing any of the following:

- market positioning
- career development
- innovation
- human resources
- customer service
- community outreach
- social media

Many people (though not nearly enough) engage in some kind of self-evaluation around New Year's, for obvious reasons. Others get inspired along the way and form a vision. So it is quite possible that you have given some thought to strategic moves that encapsulate what you want to see happening in the near future. But have you seriously planned the specific actions that will be needed to achieve those objectives?

Make some meaningful time now to review and evaluate the success of your actions and their alignment with your overall vision. Schedule on your calendar an hour to two hours this week to identify how successful your strategy has been. If no such strategy exists, this will be the time to create one. The sessions in this book will support you in ensuring your strategy serves you well.

**Who is the CEO of your endeavor?
Is it time to fire the CEO?**

Session 2

REDUCE THE RISK THAT YOUR VISION WILL END UP IN A DRAWER

What happens when your vision takes the form of a strategy to be implemented throughout a quarter, a year, or even a much longer time period? Reviewing your plan periodically is critical to staying focused and producing results that are in line with your vision.

Without a meaningful review deadline, you can spend all the time you want planning, but life will always get in the way. You come to the end of the period realizing how far off you are from manifesting your vision. You might as well have put the plan with your vision in a back drawer.

Some of my clients have asked me how often they should engage in reviewing their strategy and their vision. I'm not referring to a daily to-do list. Instead, review time is when you do the following:

- Evaluate plan progress.
- Identify delays and challenges.
- Discover resources you may need to reach out to.
- Make adjustments to your plan.

The more complex and involved your plan is, the more frequently you will need to engage in review. If others (employees, vendors, etc.) are involved in implementing your plan, make sure they are aware of your adjustments, or even become part of your evaluation process.

I have worked with managers who incorporated a monthly review and were able to maintain a high-level view, understand the details, and adjust resources in a timely manner. In some cases, a biweekly review did the trick, because more people and resources were involved. One way or another, do not go more than a quarter without taking a high-level view of your strategy.

Use your vision as a beacon. At the end of each review, ask yourself: If I continue to do what I've done so far, how much closer will I get to my vision? If the answer doesn't satisfy you, it's time to work with a professional and get some leverage on yourself.

Is your vision working for you right now?

Session 3

DON'T CONFUSE YOUR STRATEGY WITH A CHECKLIST

Many professionals spend a big portion of their time paying attention to daily issues. It's normal to create a checklist of all the items you need to accomplish during a workday or workweek. A checklist is not only helpful, it's encouraging. Many people experience that moment of great satisfaction when they cross an item off the list, so go ahead and use it.

Be aware, though, that just working off a list might give you a false feeling of being productive, while what you're really doing is replacing productivity with activity. In other words, to what extent do your daily activities (that you happily check off of your list) move you forward toward the goals that matter to you most?

The limitations of your checklist will be reduced when you are mindful of the makeup of it. The real art of the checklist is to ensure that at least 50 percent of your daily activities are tied directly to your strategy. This week, carve out an hour of your time to review your big picture. Work with someone you trust to bounce ideas off and discuss challenges. Bring your last few checklists for reference. And start asking:

- What am I doing that most effectively impacts my goals?
- What activities distract me from staying true to the strategy I've set?
- What's not working nearly as well as I'd like?
- Where do I need more help to get the right things done right?

Are the activities you checked off today part of a strategy you have defined?

Session 4

DO YOU TEND TO SET UNREALISTIC GOALS?

For many people, the start of a new year is a time for personal reflection. You may find yourself joining the 45 percent of Americans who make a New Year's resolution.[1] It is quite common to share these resolutions during celebratory events on December 31. Everyone is always in a great mood, and you become energized—not only from the support and the acknowledgment everyone gives, but also from the overall excitement that a new year brings.

It's the perfect time to aim for new highs on a business level as well as a personal level. You might decide, for example, to increase revenue by 15 percent. But are you sharing with your friends the goals that you already know are simple enough to achieve, or are you committing to goals that are so out of your comfort zone that two weeks into the year, you'll be trying to forget you ever made them?

A while back, a business owner told me, "We were working to accomplish a sales goal that was set by a consultant at the beginning of the year. We couldn't keep up with it because it wasn't really our goal."

Only 8 percent of people who make New Year's resolutions are successful in accomplishing them—and at least one out of four doesn't make it to the end of the first two weeks![2] One of the main reasons for this is because people set unrealistic goals. To make things

---

[1] Nancy Anderson, "Six Ways to Make Your New Year's Resolutions Stick In 2016," *Forbes*, December 26, 2015, http://www.forbes.com/sites/nancyanderson/2015/12/26/six-ways-to-make-your-new-years-resolutions-stick-in-2016/#541b89761f90; "New Years Resolution Statistics," Statistics Brain, December 27, 2015, http://www.statisticbrain.com/new-years-resolution-statistics/.

[2] "New Years Resolution Statistics," Statistics Brain, December 27, 2015, http://www.statisticbrain.com/new-years-resolution-statistics/.

even more challenging, setting goals is frequently done without access to proper tools and methods that can increase effectiveness and consistency in following what you truly wish.

Don't set goals for the new year on a whim. Have some method to your madness. If you want to increase your chances of accomplishing what's important to you in a specific time frame, be it a year or a quarter, invest some meaningful time in learning how to set the right goals and develop a strategy to overcome anticipated obstacles. There are many goal-setting programs on the market[3]—you just need to find the one that matches your needs.

Are you aiming too high or too low?

---

[3] The Round Well offers home-study courses like "Goal-Setting 101: How to Use Your Purpose to Raise the Bar," which you can undertake at your own convenience. It is used for setting personal goals as well as for establishing business goals. Check out http://theroundwell.com/leadership-coaching-programs/.

Session 5

DECIDE WHAT TO MEASURE

How do you know if your business is doing better than before? Traditionally, success has been measured in terms of leads, sales, income statements, and balance sheets. These measurements are easy to use and easy to track. They're a core part of your organization's performance, which is why they're referred to as key performance indicators (KPI). Are you familiar with your KPIs?

While businesses track these numbers by default (for both practical and legal reasons), these figures don't tell the whole picture. What additional indicators measure the health of an organization? Employee turnover and customer retention are a good place to start. They're pretty easy to track. They tell a story about your business's ability to serve its people and to foster a culture of loyalty.

Speaking of culture, the trouble is that other indicators that are just as important to the health of your organization are much harder to measure. Spend some time considering how to track the following:

- systematic interpersonal communication failures across your organization
- the impact of poor management on your organization
- the ripple effect of draining employees on team productivity

Knowing all of your organization's relevant KPIs allows you to evaluate areas of business based on standards and trends. So set up a mechanism—maybe a spreadsheet or software tools—to track not only revenue, sales, referrals, and customer retention but also employee turnover and culture.

If you don't track performance indicators, your ability to improve and grow your business is marginalized. What can be measured can be improved.

What are the five most important performance indicators in your business?

Session 6

SET DEADLINES ON LONG-LOST PROJECTS

It's perfectly normal to have a long to-do list and then not get to important or valuable projects because you're focused on doing all the easy or urgent stuff. This kind of problem shows up a lot when your important projects are not urgent. Because delaying has no serious consequences, it's natural to push off non-urgent but important projects unless you define a "by when"—that is, a deadline.

All major projects in corporate America follow timetables, which include milestones and estimated completion dates. At the same time, it's common to skip out on setting deadlines in more informal settings, like when you're planning your own work or your small team's work, or when you're rolling with the punches.

Here is the tricky part. A lot of people avoid setting a formal deadline because it scares the hell out of them. What if they miss it? Could they bear the thought they had failed? By focusing on the possibility that you might fail and working around it, you actually move further away from completing your project on time. Instead, focus on how meaningful a timely completion would be. Remember that deadlines are designed to protect, not to attack.

What are some of your organization's projects that have not progressed for at least a month? Maybe there was no deadline, maybe the deadline has passed, or maybe you knew that you were not going to be able to finish it as quickly as you originally thought. If you need to adjust the deadline, go ahead and do that. Communicate to all interested parties, set milestones on your calendar, assign resources to get it done, and start to pay attention when each milestone draws close.

Which milestone do you need to keep your focus on in the next week?

Session 7

GET READY FOR GROWTH

It is a well-known fact that growth requires investment. Let's say you already have a concept, a product, or a service—and you even have customers who are pleased with what you have to offer. So you figure that now is the time to expand your business.

Whether you have investors backing you up or are using your own seed money, it is wise to determine exactly where you'll be spending that money. Watch out for the following snares that often trip up business expansions:

- Most of the money goes into developing a superior product or acquiring top-of-the-line equipment, so there is very little left to tackle other challenges.
- Marketing and branding take a backseat to uncoordinated advertising.
- Staff members are not ready for expansion.

A key factor for accelerated growth is having the right people on your team. When I say "right people," I mean not only qualified technical people but also potential leaders. Great leaders are the essence of growth. They can make decisions, deal with uncertainties, take initiative, motivate others, and challenge the assumptions around growth. Answering questions like the following will help you avoid problems in the areas above:

- What will be the impact of having the latest piece of equipment without the resources to integrate it into a smooth operation? How do I convince customers of the benefits they could attain from it?

- When was the last time I reviewed my overall marketing strategy?
- Would my team and infrastructure be able to support this projected growth?

As part of your big-picture planning, you will need to identify the gap in your existing resources, outline the kind of talent you require for growth in your own business, and review your strategy with a professional.

Are you planning for growth?

Session 8

DO YOU REALLY WANT THAT CHANGE?

You're finally starting to move gently toward your annual goals, and you've discovered that holding on to your commitments is not such an easy task. You might have initiated those big moves thinking that change would be easy. But whether you wanted to implement a new sales process to attract new clients, adopt some healthier habits, or take steps to improve any other business area, at some point you will be hit by the reality of these challenges.

To embrace the change[4] more easily, do the following:

- Stay tuned to your reasons. Ask yourself why you wanted to make that change from the get-go. If you are clear about that, a dose of perseverance is required.
- Speak to your support system about your challenges. Find a friend, a mentor, a coach, or someone who simply believes in you, and together revisit your timeline.
- Acknowledge your progress.

At the same time, you'll want to avoid doing the following:

- listening to people who tell you that no one accomplishes their annual goals, just like with New Year's resolutions.
- dismissing your own goals because they are hard to achieve.

Are you ready for the change that's coming?

---

[4] To learn how to embrace change more effectively, read our latest blog post "When is The Perfect Time For a Change?" at http://theroundwell. com/when-perfect-time-for-change/.

Session 9

FIND WHAT YOU'RE MISSING

Did you know that every army operation must be followed by a debriefing? The participants go over the details with a fine-tooth comb to examine what worked and what didn't. The whole process is considered a lesson-learned opportunity, so that when the next operation takes place, they can avoid mistakes and repeat successful actions.

As mindful business owners wrap up the business year, they engage in a similar process. A true year-end evaluation, or something similar at the end of a major initiative, is needed not only to identify successes but also to pinpoint opportunities that didn't materialize.

Some individuals choose to quickly move on to setting up new goals for the new year before addressing what was not accomplished. I am all for setting goals, and I help people do that in a smart way. Nonetheless, it is just as strategic to learn from what was not accomplished. What can you learn? A ton!

Here is your warning: refrain from blaming others. It may be easy and simple, but it's also completely ineffective. Although others may have contributed to your results, the one thing you have definite control over is yourself. If those opportunities were presented to you, you had something to do with how they did or did not materialize.

If you are open to learning something significant about yourself, you can get to the core of achieving all the future goals you'll ever set.

Schedule some quiet and uninterrupted time to do your own debrief. Review various opportunities that came your way and ask yourself the following questions:

- Did I seek out opportunities but then find convenient reasons not to take advantage of them?

- Did I see opportunities and move on to take action to seize the moment as soon as possible?
- Did I see opportunities and get stuck in paralysis-by-analysis until it was too late?

Even if year-end is far away, make sure you benefit from this process. Schedule your quiet time to debrief the last quarter or the latest project.

Being honest with yourself may be the best thing you can do to avoid repeating mistakes.

Are you ready to do some searching?

Session 10

PRACTICE MAKES PERFECT?

You have probably heard the phrase "practice makes perfect." This means you need to keep practicing in order to get better at math, music, sports, and whatever else you take on.

There are plenty of books that explain that the difference between professionals and amateurs is the sheer length of time required (10,000 hours) to reach a professional level in anything you do. Putting the time in is necessary but not in itself sufficient. Repetition has limitations.

Let's say you want to improve your sales, or you want to enhance your customer retention. In other words, you want to perfect your game in a specific area. What if you continue doing exactly the same thing over and over again? Is there any chance you'll see a change in your results?

In order to make something perfect, you have to evaluate it frequently and adjust your practice. Any evaluation process should therefore contain the following steps:

1. Review your results and any leading statistics.
2. Learn new business and market conditions.
3. Review your methods and their success rate.
4. Learn about relevant alternatives.
5. Decide which alternatives you can integrate in your practice.

Then put the necessary time into practicing, and evaluate it all again. In my work with business owners, I've found that a quarterly review can provide enough data to begin a serious evaluation.

**What are you taking on yourself to make
perfect in your business or in your life?**

Session 11

HELP YOUR BUSINESS SURVIVE WITHOUT YOU

Late this summer, I had to put down my pen, contact my clients to reschedule all sessions, and literally walk away from my office for quite a while. The other alternative was to continue business as usual and not attend to my dad's situation. He was hospitalized abroad at the time. I made up my mind and quickly packed. I knew in my heart that I had made a sound decision. Yet during the extremely long flight, my mind was racing with the dilemma of how my business would function if I had to be away for a longer period of time.

Whether you're a business owner, an independent producer, or a manager, your presence has a direct impact on the results you achieve. Have you ever prepared to leave? I invite you to read my blog post on "How to Prepare for a Long Departure"[5] and brainstorm about how you can be prepared for that day when you may need to put your family first.

How would your business function if you had to be away for longer than a casual vacation?

---

[5] Find it at http://theroundwell.com/succession-planning-long-departure/.

Session 12

CONSIDER REALLOCATING YOUR RESOURCES

When year-end comes around, it is common (and advisable) to go over your budget, review your year-to-date numbers, and make a forecast for the year to come. Some businesses project revenue based on trends in the market together with their previous year's performance. This method puts them in a reactive mode for the coming year.

How about using a more proactive approach and making some decisions that will affect next year's performance? Although annual trends in your market indicate where your business may be heading, your revenue forecast could be based on actions you are planning to take that translate into the manpower and dollar resources you'll be allocating.

In order to put yourself in the driver's seat, ask yourself the following questions:

- Do I spend the same money in the same business areas as I did in the past?
- Do I allocate resources to different business areas that could really shift the direction of the business next year?
- What expenditures are intended to increase my customer base or boost capacity?
- Have I had extensive success with prior expense categories, or was the return barely acceptable?

Make sure to consider any new activities or new business areas that allow for results that were not possible before because there has been a change in the marketplace.

There are plenty of new activities that can generate future revenues, but if you continue to use the same old approach, you resort to playing catch-up with what others are already implementing and perfecting. A more proactive projection model helps your business become more dynamic in today's market.

McKinsey and Company's extensive research[6] suggests that resource reallocation is a muscle that requires exercise in good times and even more in bad times. Companies should be on their guard against inertia. Usually, corporations present a favorable bottom line to their shareholders as a result of increase in performance.

What would an increase in your business performance mean to you?

---

[6] McKinsey and Company conducted large-scale research of reallocation patterns of multi-business companies in October of 2013. The research shows that the performance of those companies that hardly reshuffled their resources was lower than the performance of companies who reallocated their resources over the years. See http://www.mckinsey.com/business-functions/strategy-and-corporate-finance/our-insights/never-let-a-good-crisis-go-to-waste.

Session 13

ARE YOU LOSING MONEY?

You're probably familiar with the idea of a cost center. It's an area where your business only indirectly generates revenue, like marketing, purchasing, or administration. Cost centers help your company, but sometimes it's hard to see how, and this presents a problem. When you need to cut costs, there may be places where it seems easiest to make savings, but without verification you can end up cutting an area that is delivering a lot of added benefit.

It's important to know which activities deliver the most value to the bottom line ... and which ones don't. Do you know where you should cut cost? This week, find the top three areas where you're spending a lot of money *and* where the exact impact on your bottom line isn't immediately clear.

Then ask a hell of a lot of questions, like the following:

- What is the added value these activities bring?
- In what way do they make our line of work more simple ... or more complex?
- What is at risk if we stop these activities altogether?
- What if we only scale down the cost but don't cut it altogether?

You may be surprised by your answers.

Please note, I'm not saying you have to stop at three activities. If you are on a roll, you can look at the next few high-ticket items. I recommend coming back and revisiting this exercise once a quarter.

What are the top activities you are about to investigate?

Session 14

GEAR UP FOR RESULTS

Do you remember a time when you had to finish up a huge project at school? You may have worked long hours, pulled all-nighters, or even hustled in the nick of time to tie all the loose ends together, because missing an imminent deadline meant you'd either fail the course or barely get a passing grade.

Fortunately, not all projects you take on will have such stringent conditions. Phew! What a relief! And yet without that strict looming outcome of a fail or a pass, you may find it challenging to see a complex undertaking all the way through to completion.

Anytime you gear up for new accomplishments, therefore, you'll want to pay close attention to your own performance. Once you set your mind on accomplishing an important project, consider not only having a winning mind-set but also taking steps that will lead to a favorable outcome. The following are some proven methods that successful leaders use over and again when they tackle huge ventures:

- Keep the big picture in mind.
- Track details that are affecting the result, even if their significance is not yet clear.
- Monitor conditions and events impacting the success of the project.
- Be persistent! Don't give up when challenges arise, just because they are challenges.

- Evaluate each and every factor that seems to indicate that it may be time to let go of the project.
- Establish an accountability partner with whom you can share your progress. If this structure becomes loose, work with a professional.

Where could having a determined mind-set help you next?

PART 2

REINVENTING YOUR PROCESSES

A process is a series of actions that produce something or that lead to a particular result. Every business operation is comprised of a handful of processes. These could be routine actions that follow a written procedure or practices that take place once in a blue moon. Effective processes help you create strong value and increase your profits. Lack of processes to follow guarantees inconsistency.

Session 15

WHY ARE YOU HAVING DELAYS?

Have you ever wondered if your team or your customers experience unreasonable delays getting results in a timely manner? When customers reach out to an institution and sense procrastination on the other end, that increases their level of frustration. The risk of either losing that customer or getting a bad review increases. And it's not just customers who get frustrated. Anyone can experience chronic delays in process, even within the same company.

Don't assume that red tape is a phenomenon limited to government agencies—it's not. This annoyance can afflict any business where there is lack of information, indecisiveness, unclear definition of responsibility, and concentration of decision-making power in one place. The impact of a bottleneck to your business could be emotional as well as financial.

It is worthwhile to take five and figure out where in your business an unnecessary time lag can occur. When you take time to explore, it is important to identify the reason for the bottleneck in order to address it. Your investigation could include the following questions:

- Do we do things in the right order?
- Can we add another step or modify an earlier step that will provide necessary data?
- Do we have the right people involved in the decision?
- Do we see that one specific employee delays decisions?

When a bottleneck is identified as one of your team members, make sure you ask that individual the following:

- Do you have all the information you need to accomplish this task? What's missing?
- Do you feel fully capable of making this happen? Why or why not?

What factors impact your need to hold back the process?

Session 16

GAIN FROM IMPLEMENTING TECHNOLOGY

Business owners seek to implement new technology so that they can improve productivity, increase efficiency, enhance safety, collect valuable information about their customers, or stay ahead of the game by offering new and improved services. Once a project is done, its primary advocate wears it like a badge of honor. Why not? It takes a tremendous amount of effort and capital to introduce new technology.

In the many years I was heading technology projects in corporate America, I noticed over and over again how much time was dedicated to not only putting the new technology in place but also to re-engineering the way people got their job done with the new tools. This is part of a bigger initiative called *process improvement*. That's where the real money is being saved. Just having cutting-edge technology handy brings little value, and many times it creates resentment in your employees.

Can you imagine buying a smartphone at full price and using it exactly the same way as you used phones a decade ago—just to make phone calls? The key in establishing the value of a technology is in the alignment of roles and responsibilities with the new capabilities you implement. It is not the job of your employees to figure it out. If you want to ensure that your business gains the benefits you intended from the new technology, ask yourself the following:

- What was the newest technology I implemented in the last twelve months?
- Does it do for my business what I had hoped for when I decided to purchase it?

- How much more can my business gain if I ensure my staff really take advantage of the technology the way I imagined?

Work with a professional who, knowing your overall direction, can ensure that you indeed improve processes and reap savings.

Are you ready to wear that badge of honor and go beyond the technical edge?

Session 17

REMOVE BARRIERS TO CREATIVITY

The search for innovation is necessary not only for survival but also for the growth of your business. As a result of continual innovation, new elements are introduced into our daily lives.

In the course of a normal day, I meet with businesspeople who are required to solve problems on an ongoing basis. Who isn't? One of the most helpful skills at their disposal is their ability to engage in innovation. It seems that innovation is required for advanced problem solving, for staying on the cutting edge, and for delivering solutions to changing markets. But what does innovation mean?

Innovation is about creating new ideas or synthesizing ideas to make new solutions.

Do you have to be born with creativity? Actually, not at all. You can practice visioning and focusing so you become skilled at getting outside of your comfort zone to create something new. Interestingly enough, the formal education system has only started to integrate creativity in its curriculum through assessments and exercises in schools. That being said, you may view yourself as barely creative—or not creative at all.

As adults, we are hardly aware of the thoughts and activities that bind our minds. It's time to reassess how creative you can really be. If you aspire to create new things, your first task is to be aware of what is in your way so you can strategize how to overcome that. The top three barriers to creativity in business are

- fear of the new,
- inertia, and
- bureaucracy.

What is the biggest hurdle to your own creativity in business?

Session 18

DOCUMENT YOUR PROCESSES

How many times have you started to work on something like filling out important paperwork, setting up features on software, or even recalibrating equipment, and to your frustration you couldn't remember exactly how you did it the last time? It is quite possible that it's only seldom that you repeat this specific task, and that is the exact reason your slick memory hasn't sprung into gear.

The knowledge that you already accomplished that task in the past may provide some relief. And yet not remembering all the details at that moment means you have to utilize trial and error ... all over again. The immediate result is a waste of time and irritation over this unnecessary laboring.

But the picture is even bleaker if you think that you may have to repeat this task in the future. Each time you go through this same process, your sense of failure increases. Furthermore, even if you decide to hand the task over to someone else, would you even be able to explain the details to ensure it's done properly?

Fortunately, there is a way out. When you acknowledge the level of effort required, start taking notes. Although you may feel that this slows down the process, it's exactly what is needed to help you next time—or when you decide to delegate the chore to someone else.

What are the functions in your line of work that you need to document correctly?

Session 19

PREVENT INFORMATION OVERLOAD

Have you ever found yourself immersed in an article that was utterly insignificant to your strategic direction? Or getting sucked into a current attention-grabbing media-generated crisis that will mean nothing in a week? Have you ever felt overwhelmed and uncertain you'll ever have enough time to follow up on important trends? Do you look at tons of details on a daily basis and try to decipher what's important to your job and what's not?

Many managers feel that they must catch up on every detail in the media—and catch up quickly! However, it's impossible to analyze and digest the enormous amount of information around you in a timely manner. In order to minimize the job, consider the following tactics:

- Use tools like Readability to mark articles in topics that your business depends on, for a later reading, so you can stay focused on daily operations.
- Allocate reading time in your weekly schedule.
- Partner with professionals who would be happy to share with you those tidbits of data that are truly relevant to your long-term strategy, so you can spend time reading only the executive summary.

This week, make time to figure out what's important to you, your career, your business, and your life. Once you do that, ask yourself the following:

- What are the three to five critical topics that impact my business?

- Who are some experts I can rely on to sift through information, present me with highlights, and refer me to more details if I need them?

**What's the real mission-critical stuff
you need to stay abreast of?**

Session 20

READY FOR THE SURVIVAL OF THE FITTEST?

Since the dawn of creation, human beings and other species have had to adapt to changes in order to survive. Each decade brings changes to our business environment at an increasing rate. In order to thrive, not just survive, we need to adjust to different conditions.

Surprisingly, many people are reluctant to adapt. It is much easier to stick to what you've always done than to risk trying something else. But what if familiarity comes at the price of running down your career or business? Your question becomes: what kind of change am I required to take?

If you want to focus on your true intention to thrive, pay attention to the most simplistic format for change. If you are not ready, reading the rest of this section will not make a difference. So here it is:

- Identify the three most unproductive actions you take on a regular basis.
- Kiss them good-bye.

You may ask: "What about the results of these actions?" Let me explain. Those unproductive tasks either did not get the results you wanted or had a negative impact in other areas. In any case, it is not worth doing it *that way*, which means something needs to change.

Is that all? Absolutely not! As Winston Churchill said, "To improve is to change; to be perfect is to change often."

Every so often, continue to identify what you need to stop doing, possibly with the help of others who actively support your progress. Soon enough, you'll be looking for new and improved ways of accomplishing what seemed far-fetched in the past.

What are the three most unproductive actions you take on a regular basis?

Session 21

LOOK INTO YOUR CRYSTAL BALL

Established corporations have professionals dedicated to integrating new thinking into the development of new products. They are called futurists.[7] With the help of futurists, products such as SmartGauge and Brake Coach were conceived to help "conscious drivers" change their driving behaviors and maximize fuel efficiency. Conscious drivers are a growing segment of the population. The result: these products gain greater customer appreciation and increase market share.

Does the futurist have a crystal ball? Of course not. But futurists do have specific ways of thinking that you may want to incorporate. To help you discover your next service or product, do the following:

- Welcome new ideas.
- Listen to your customers' needs, especially when they indicate that your current service is lacking.
- Ask tons of questions to understand what could benefit your customers.
- Review with your team examples from a variety of industries to identify any new population and economic trends.
- Brainstorm to consider what problems need to be solved for these population segments.

---

[7] Jeff Chu, "Sheryl Connelly: The Car Clairvoyant," *Fast Company,* May 13, 2013, www.fastcompany.com/3009210/most-creative-people-2013/24-sheryl-connelly.

If you are seeking growth, it isn't enough to focus on the services you offer currently. It's time to think forward. You do not need to be an official inventor to have a forward-thinking process in your business.

When is the next time you plan
to talk about the future?

Session 22

CONSIDER A MAKEOVER

Plenty of actions you take work really well. Those activities helped you produce your current accomplishments. You've done it for a while. You are comfortable making it happen again. Nonetheless, when you desire new results, you may wonder: Is that enough?

Whether you want to venture into a new career, create a new service, increase your company's market share, or change an industry from the core, the actions leading to the results you desire are probably outside your comfort zone. You may need to redesign your business, reinvent yourself, and possibly both. One indication of a necessary business redesign is a feeling of stagnation. Sometimes you don't even need to look at quarters after quarters of financial results.

Many people feel threatened by the thought of reinventing themselves out of the sheer fear of possible failure. When it comes to redesigning a business, you must accept that you are walking toward the unknown. Only a few consider that with enthusiasm. The following are key factors to help you set yourself up for a successful redesign process:

- Consider that you can learn from every failure.
- Use your human support structure.
- Leave your ego at the door.
- Act with full intention.
- Be open-minded.

Next time you consider doing a makeover, in order to access results you've never achieved, know that you are already fantastic and that you can only make yourself better following the above principles. As Jason Wilson, the lead product designer of Pinterest, is quoted as saying, "A redesign is not about ego. It's about taking a fantastic ... and making it better."

Are you comfortable with the results you generate?

Session 23

SIMPLIFY YOUR MEETINGS

Meetings are one area where it's easy to get off track, lose valuable time, and avoid or ignore pressing issues that merit group discussion. So what's the difference between an effective meeting and an ineffective one? Oftentimes, success boils down to a single piece of paper called an agenda.

If you're going to spend the time to call a meeting, take a few minutes to prepare an agenda. What are the topics you need to cover? Put them on the agenda. Who do you need to hear from? Any status to be reported? Put it on the agenda. Review all the topics that you think are important to cover and allocate time accordingly.

Send anyone who is going to the meeting a copy of the agenda a day in advance, or at least a few hours ahead. Bring enough copies to distribute to everyone, plus a few extra. That way, you save time, keep the meeting going in an orderly fashion, and bring a high degree of thoroughness to the topics presented. Talk about an easy efficiency hack.

What is the main topic of your next meeting?

Session 24

KEEP EVOLVING

Have you noticed the leaves turning color in the fall? Fall is a beautiful time to appreciate gorgeous foliage ... but there are actually some interesting mechanisms in the background we can learn from for our business.

For trees, each leaf is an energy factory. When a leaf shrivels and falls, production shuts down. That's part of a biological system that regulates change. The tree gets feedback on what's going on outside and adjusts as necessary to keep its operations efficient. Millions of years of evolution have honed this process to perfection, and getting feedback from the environment is key to keeping the cycle alive.

So here are the million-dollar questions to ask yourself:

- What method of feedback do I employ in my business?
- Where can I use feedback to improve my operation?
- How often am I getting new information about what's working, not working, or not working as well as I'd like?
- Who am I counting on to give me the kind of feedback I really need?

Who you can invite to have a face-to-face or virtual chat on this topic?

Session 25

INCREASE CLARITY, EFFICIENCY, AND EFFECTIVENESS

As a business owner or a manager, your day gets filled up with numerous tasks. Sometimes, at the end of the week, it may seem unclear what you have accomplished.

Sure, you do a lot of things. But have you asked yourself, "Do I do the things that will further my objectives?" Or "Am I working in the most efficient way?"

Some people use checklists to track all their tasks. That's great. If you're one of those people, how's that working for you? What sense of achievement do you get from looking at your checklist? What's missing for many is time to address those questions and look at things from a different perspective.

When you make the time to plan your work, you get clear on where you are heading. If you are not sure about that, revisit Part 1 of this book. When you plan, you get to see how you can create and work smarter. Having clarity allows you to build your to-do list so it is based on what is really important instead of just checking off items and doing busy work.

During your review time, evaluate your progress and make adjustments. This allows for increasing both efficiency and effectiveness. Obviously, a review-plan session is not a one-off thing. Each objective requires a different frequency of review-plan sessions. The more frequent they are, the higher the possibility of correcting course and of achieving a sense of accomplishment.

What frequency works best for you?

Session 26

BREAK OUT OF STAGNATION

You must have heard the phrase, "If it's not broken, don't fix it." Do you believe it?

It's common for small companies to not focus on innovation or continuous improvement. Operation is based on doing things "the way we always did." The reason many managers support this approach is because it's a reflection of their comfort zone.

However, the comfort zone invites stagnation. If stagnation is present and the company is challenged by its competitors, the management team will, at best, scramble to react because the threat came at them out of left field. Some big corporations falter because they're so busy following procedure that they fail to pursue new opportunities at the low end of their markets.

To recognize the best opportunities, you first need to view the status quo as insufficient. In other words, make continuous improvement mandatory. And where do you start? Make time to brainstorm. Engage a task force or call a meeting with key employees to discuss how you can break out of stagnation periodically. Here are some questions to brainstorm with your team:

- Can you think of any place in our company where we stick to the status quo instead of identifying improvements?
- Where are we satisfied with the way things are instead of the way they can be?
- Where do we overlook opportunities for growth or profit?

When can you schedule your next brainstorm session?

Session 27

GIVE YOURSELF A TIME-OUT

When you find yourself dealing with problem after problem, you may start to become overwhelmed and think "This is all I can do: solve problems."

When sport coaches call a time-out, they want a game changer. You may wonder, "How does that relate to me?" It's time for a game changer in your business so you will stop selling yourself short.

The human mind is a fabulous tool. When it quiets down, the creative part can easily join the logical part. Your whole mind encompasses the best in you. Make sure you take time out of your day to slow down and let your mind get quiet. Only a few minutes of clearing your mind will allow you to assess your situation.

This type of high-level thinking allows you not only to resolve problems more efficiently or avoid them altogether but also to address those things that are waiting to happen "one day." On top of that, it allows you to come up with new ideas, new solutions, and new innovations, all related to improving the way you get things done. Take a moment a day to slow down and think.

What is the best reason for you to take a time-out today?

Session 28

CREATE YOUR FUTURE

Let's assume you just took your time-out. Sometimes thoughts of things that already happened cross your mind, and all you do is think of the past. Other times, you may feel somewhat hopeful, and you can then start to look ahead.

As you open yourself to new opportunities, you may want to ask yourself, "Can only an external opportunity create something different for me? Or can it be me?"

You can wait for things to happen and have no say in the matter, or you can be the catalyst for what the future will hold.

Consider changing your attitude and changing your game. It's time for you to create opportunities in your business, your career, and your life.

How can you do things differently, so you can create new opportunities in the future?

PART 3

HANDLING YOUR EMPLOYEES' CHALLENGES

If you had ideal employees, they would do everything just like you imagined. In reality, that is far from the case. That is why employees present big challenges to business owners—not because they plan to be difficult, but because their minds work differently from yours.

Session 29

PREPARE YOUR NEW EMPLOYEES

A long time ago—and I will not divulge how long ago it was—I showed up to my first day of work at a great company located in one of the skyscrapers of Manhattan. I was excited and ready to put myself to work so I could show them who I was.

It was quite intriguing to observe that not everything was ready for me. My workstation, my ID, and my connection to the company databases and software—as well as some other logistical issues—were all delayed. I was scheduled to attend an orientation session within a few days, and until then it looked like the company trusted that I would catch up on what was going on from a few of my peers and the manager, who was busy running the project. Within hours, my enthusiasm diminished.

As much as I would like to believe otherwise, this is not uncommon. I have heard similar stories of how employers missed great opportunities when hiring new blood. If you are on the other side of the hiring spectrum, there is a crucial lesson to learn from this practice. Every manager and business owner wants new hires to hit the ground running. No wonder, given that they spend a considerable amount of time selecting someone with the necessary skills and attitude.

The first day on location is a crucial day. Newly hired employees are full of energy and excitement. They want to prove themselves to you and to themselves. At this critical time, you need to be focused on integrating them with your business operation, not only for that day but also for the future of a healthy employee-employer relationship.

So what can you do when you hire new employees, engage

subcontractors to work on a project for you, or even bring in seasonal help? Start with the following:

- Set up the needed logistics (including tools and access) ahead of their start time.
- Outline your expectations clearly.
- Give them all the information they need to start, and direct them to a library of resources where they can find additional documentation specific to your business.
- Spend one-on-one time to tell them about the core values of your team that are important to the future of your business.
- Introduce them to a team contact person, preferably a mentor or yourself, and make sure both schedule follow-up time to meet.

The bottom line is that new hires need your direction even if they came with impressive recommendations. They cannot get into your head. Make sure you share what's important to you and make it a procedure to follow every time you hire.

And what if your hired a new employee a few weeks ago and you haven't done all of the above? Simple. Do it this week.

How can you make your new employees feel welcome?

Session 30

SET YOUR PEOPLE UP TO WIN

Some of your employees are highly competent but aren't performing as well as you'd like them to. They may do a great job in many other areas of their lives, but they sure aren't bringing high performance to their day job. So what's getting in their way?

Gallup, Inc., conducted extensive research involving 80,000 managers across different industries, and this is what they found: in order for employees to perform at their peak, a company must satisfy their basic needs first. What are these basic needs?

- knowing what is expected at work
- having the equipment and support to do work the right way
- receiving appropriate praise and feedback for the work accomplished

A common mistake for business owners is to think that, "By now, my employees should just get it." But if your employees don't act like they got it, they didn't get it. Understand that your employees can't read your mind. Start communicating your expectations in a way that is 100 percent clear. Have them repeat back to you what they understood. Don't just ask: "Do you understand?"

Some managers tend to talk a lot. It is necessary to focus what you say on the important stuff. Frequently review to see if there is anything employees lack to do their job properly and ensure it is being replenished or addressed. Make sure the feedback you provide to underperforming employees gives them the information they need to fix the problem.

What would be the most important thing to say to your employees?

Session 31

STOP WAITING FOR THE RIGHT MOMENT

Do you remember a time when you realized that you needed to convey an important message to one of your team members, and yet somehow you didn't? You might want to talk to people from time to time for one of the following reasons:

- Their attendance has started to be inconsistent.
- Their attention to details has declined and a project was underpriced.
- Their backlog has increased and started to affect additional timelines.
- Their demeanor has become sour and drains the energy of others in the workplace.

As important as these things are, you've never addressed them. And now, they seem too petty to mention, even though the behavior hasn't gone away. What's happening? Like many managers, you are waiting for the right moment, and it seems like that moment never arrives.

In speaking with clients, I've realized how many people hold back on addressing issues with their employees or even with colleagues. I can't say I'm totally surprised. What did surprise me was how long they waited until they finally took a stand and initiated a conversation.

Many times we make excuses for the other person just because we don't want to get into a conflict or we are too concerned with how the person will react. So we let it go—after all, it's just one incident. But then the behavior shows up again, and it annoys us even more. Again, we get distracted, and we don't have the time to address it.

When you do notice the same undesired behavior again, it's time to decide which of the following is more likely:

1. It's a fluke. Something did happen, but it was just a random occurrence, and your team member's performance is back to normal.
2. It's become more of a regular occurrence, almost a habit.

If the second option is true, things are not going to change while you wait for your moment, and that will drain your energy. Seize the moment to give feedback and get energized because the issue has been addressed after all this time.

What are you holding back, thinking that you need to make the time to say something?

Session 32

SHOULD YOU RETRAIN OR FIRE YOUR PROBLEM EMPLOYEES?

How do you deal with problem employees? The choice is tough, but the solutions don't have to be. We are not talking about an employee who needs a wake-up call, a serious reminder, or extra hand-holding during the early days in your business unit. Problem employees display a behavior over a period of time that presents them as aggressive, unreliable, lazy, or just plain ineffective.

Employees should be an asset to your organization. They are the reason work gets done when your attention is elsewhere. Without them, you don't have much of an organization at all (at least until the robot revolution). But what do you do when an employee becomes a liability? When you can't count on an individual to get the job done at all, let alone effectively? When their behavior patterns cause harm or have the potential to cause harm (maybe even involving litigation)?

When things get to this point, you have the following options:

- You can do nothing, ignore the problem, and hope the consequences will be minimal.
- You can address problem behaviors through training.
- You can let the employee go.

From years of working with my coaching clients, I understand that business owners feel connected and responsible not only to their employees but also to their employees' families. They try to avoid a decision that might affect family members. So unfortunately, the first option is the most used one. And yet by shifting focus to personal issues, they fail to see how a long-term negative involvement may affect the business overall and eventually everyone involved—including employees and their families.

It's important to consider also which option is more likely to reduce your liability, and which would best help to increase the performance of the whole team. Make sure that you discuss the possibilities with a professional. Sometimes, it is important to get help navigating through this type of challenge—only because, when it comes to people, our judgments become clouded with emotions.

Are you ready to make some tough choices?

Session 33

DO YOU HAVE TO PAY MORE TO ENSURE EMPLOYEE SATISFACTION?

I stumbled upon some interesting statistics in a Society for Human Resource Management survey[8] the other day and found that the top two factors contributing to employee job satisfaction since 2002 are not what you might think. Although some may say that money moves the world around, compensation has not been the top factor throughout a whole decade that included a major economic downturn. The following are the top contributors:

- opportunities to use skills and abilities
- job security

The next factors in line are:

- compensation
- communication between employees and senior management
- relationship with immediate supervisor

That shines a different light on a thought I hear from some of my clients: *Well, if I raise my employees' salary, they would be more satisfied.*

Now, wait a second. Was there an implied correlation between pay increase and increase in job satisfaction?

Don't get me wrong, raises are important to retaining high-caliber

---

[8] Society for Human Resource Management (SHRM), *2012 Employee Job Satisfaction and Engagement: How Employees Are Dealing with Uncertainty,* https://www.shrm.org/Research/SurveyFindings/ Documents/12-0537%202012_jobsatisfaction_fnl_online.pdf.

employees. Competitive salaries are part of a package designed to attract the best, and raises help keep the best. But paying people more money does *not* make them more satisfied at work. It might keep them around longer, but it won't increase their level of engagement. It won't empower them to produce better work. It won't fix gripes they have about other unaddressed issues.

Want a consistent way to retain your best employees, beyond making sure they are compensated competitively? Try the following:

- Give them opportunities to develop.
- Instill in them a sense of purpose, fulfillment, and importance.
- Honor their contribution.
- Develop a positive culture that supports open communication.

If you have an employee who consistently focuses on pay increases, it's time to have a purposeful discussion to evaluate that individual's level of satisfaction on the job.

What are your employees looking to you for?

Session 34

CELEBRATE ACHIEVEMENTS

When is it a good time to celebrate? There's no better time to throw a big bash than when marking the accomplishment of a meaningful project.

Okay—maybe throwing a big party is going a little overboard. What I'm really talking about isn't just ordering pizza to the office, nor is it planning a sleek black-tie affair. Instead, your focus should be on identifying accomplishments worth celebrating with your team.

Perhaps it's a new system you installed that is now online, humming along without additional effort. It could be a big sale someone in your organization just landed or a record number of returning customers. There are lots of things happening in your business every day, and most of them are invisible (because we tend to focus on the problems). But there's plenty of stuff to acknowledge.

How you celebrate is entirely up to you. Maybe just taking ten minutes to appreciate the good work done is enough. Other possibilities include arranging a team-building event onsite or offsite, or gathering the team and announcing achievements while giving a plaque or a thank-you card with a gift card or tickets for a show or a game. It really depends on the size of the achievement. The point isn't how much time or how much money you spend; rather, it's about being intentional in the way you recognize achievement.

Why? People like to be recognized. The effect of showing your appreciation goes a long way. You'll be surprised at how the sense of belonging to a celebratory effort fuels employee energy even more than receiving a paycheck.

What can you celebrate with your team this month?

Session 35

WHO'S DOING THE WORK?

Many managers think that their employees can do more. However, giving more work does not necessarily produce better results.

One way to get more out of your team is to assess the strengths of your people and then assign work that matches your employees' strengths. Take a few minutes to check in with the following:

- Are you giving the right work to the right people?
- Do your top employees seem overwhelmed?
- Do your less-skilled employees end up doing the minimum you can trust them with?
- Do your employees get tasks that are challenging or not challenging?

If you're occupying your most qualified people with work that doesn't suit them, they'll eventually become restless. Maybe they'll even be bored, while others, for whom the work would be appropriate, stay underutilized. On the other hand, if you're giving complex tasks to only the most qualified people, you lose opportunities to continue developing your less-skilled employees.

In the long run, you can end up with situations where you're depending on only the same small group of people to get the job done. The work (or the supervision of that work) may end up on your to-do list, which is the exact opposite of why you hired people in the first place.

What's your to-do list for this week?

As a personnel training exercise, hand off a semi-complex project to someone who can handle it but to whom you ordinarily would not have given that project. This may require more short-term supervision, but you'll find out whether it is a worthwhile trade-off. And you'll start mastering the art of giving work to the right people.

It's important to note that this semi-complex project doesn't have to be a project you usually do, so the person who usually is involved with the details can also have a chance of supervising a task.

Who is the lucky employee you are about to develop?

Session 36

LET SOMEONE ELSE DO IT

Do you run out of day before you run out of work? It always seems like there's so much to do and not enough resources. Well, you've got resources: people, time, money, materials, and energy. How efficiently do you allocate all that stuff?

Have you ever felt like your plate is so full that adding one more item may cause you to let go of one of your major commitments? You are in good company with a lot of my clients.

You may have even tried multitasking to address this challenge. But that didn't help to keep your head above water. And then, as you are involved with one of those "needed to get it done yesterday" tasks, you may entertain the thought: *Someone else can do it.*

As you are coming up with alternatives to free some time for more important tasks, your mind plays tricks on you with a second thought: *By the time I explain it to them, I might as well have done myself.* Letting that thought prevail leaves you endlessly overwhelmed.

When is it worth it to spend the time and explain to someone else how to do a task, so you can save time and energy and get back in control of your schedule? When any of the following conditions exists:

- The task has a straightforward outcome.
- The issue is of low risk.
- You can clearly explain the steps to get the required result.
- You do it over and over again.

Note that once you start enjoying the benefits of delegating repeated tasks, you feel more comfortable delegating tasks that may be required only once.

Which task is getting off your list right away?

Session 37

TALK TO YOUR DRAMA QUEENS

Have you ever worked with a chronic complainer? These employees may do good work on their own, but their impact on your work environment is toxic. Why? Because complaining brings your team down and drains energy. And that's a problem!

As a manager, it's important to know if there's a valid issue worth addressing. But what if there isn't? Some people just complain for the sake of complaining. People like that gradually become tuned out and isolated—or even worse, they polarize your workforce.

What do you do with chronic complainers? Your goal is to redirect the drama.

Remember—some people just need to vent. If you could help them find an effective way to vent—specifically, a way that doesn't affect workplace performance—what would be the effect? Start by offering them a more private way to vent, where someone besides another employee will hear them out, such as one of the following:

- a short conversation with a personal friend to blow off steam
- a call with a coach to deal with the issue of chronic complaining
- a discussion with you, the manager, to address a substantive issue

Who do you need to have a word with?

Session 38

MAKE YOUR COMPANY ONE THAT PEOPLE WANT TO WORK FOR

When more than 275,000 employees voice their opinion about what counts, you may want to pay attention. In an extensive survey conducted by *Fortune* magazine, employees were asked about their attitudes regarding management credibility, job satisfaction, and camaraderie. This project also reviewed benefit programs, hiring practices, methods of internal communication, training, recognition programs, and diversity efforts.

Let's go over some gems that do not require a substantial financial investment:

- Genentech (California) inspires employees with presentations by patients whose lives have been helped by their products.
- Intuit (California) encourages employees to spend 10 percent of their time at work pursuing projects they're passionate about. They also reward employees for innovations that become new products.
- At Devon Energy (Oklahoma), the CEO calls employees or sends personalized notes to thank them for a job well done.
- At Umpqua Bank (Portland), employees gather every morning for a "motivation moment" in which teams recognize achievements, play games, and set goals.

The things these companies do to become known as great employers contribute to lowering employee turnover (a huge hidden cost). Surely your company would benefit from that.

Would your employees consider you a great employer? What are some ideas you have on improving employee job satisfaction that do not require a high monetary investment? Think about your work environment and career-development opportunities, for example.

How would your company rate on that survey?

Session 39

DEEPEN YOUR TALENT POOL

When Steve Jobs built Apple, he couldn't rely solely on his own genius genes. He surrounded himself with bright and super-competent individuals who were able to focus on operations and technical design challenges to complement what he brought to the table.

The strength of your business banks on the total talent pool you can orchestrate. And to spice things up, the needed talent pool for a thriving business is a moving target. As the marketplace changes, some skills become obsolete while others emerge.

Some business owners and managers are reluctant to recruit or develop sharp employees for fear of becoming less significant themselves. When it's time to look for new employees, they look for the kind of talent they can easily manage. At times, they feel like they have to know all the details of how to get any task done so they can keep an eye on their employees' performance.

Naturally, they look for specific technical skills while ignoring people skills and potential for growth. Looking at these aspects may weed out candidates who will turn out complacent at best. More than that, when it's time to develop their employees and support their growth, they hold back, for the reasons mentioned above. The overall result is mediocre performance.

Can you handle the talent you could have? To take your business performance to the next level, you need to consciously evaluate these two aspects on an annual basis:

1. Which talents will be needed in your future company (having both skills and growth potential) so you are ready to recruit them in a timely manner?
2. How might you be able to enhance your own leadership skills so you can comfortably bring in some "big guns"?

What leadership skill do you need to strengthen?

Session 40

LEARN TO MANAGE CHAOS

Most traditional science deals with supposedly predictable phenomena. Chaos theory addresses things that are impossible to predict or control. Many business owners indicate with sadness that they don't feel in control of all aspects of their businesses.

That feeling of lack of control originates because others (their staff members or field employees) take actions and make decisions that are not in harmony with what the owners would have chosen to do. The results could be a waste of resources, inefficiency, focus in the wrong direction, growing tension in the office, mishandling of customer expectations, and so forth. But those outcomes are not inevitable.

Growth is impossible when the business owner is the bottleneck for all decisions. As a business grows, owners need to be able to count on others to make decisions and take unsupervised actions. That being said, when you start to delegate, there is one common mistake you must avoid: trusting that your employees understand where you are coming from.

When you operate under the assumption that they understand how you think they should be acting, you're going to be disappointed—because they don't!

Recognizing that others may not follow exactly the same thought pattern that you have prepares you to start managing the chaos. Your thought patterns are based on your perspective and your experiences. The same is true for others who work for you. Therefore, it is only predictable that they will take different actions from those you would take.

You can avoid this by providing structure and process to ensure the chaos is minimized. Having a set frequency for follow-ups with employees where you cover status, challenges, solutions, and an action plan is a good place to start building that structure and process.

What is one critical task that you assume your employees could do just the way you envision without you giving them specifics?

Session 41

CREATE A RESPONSIBILITY STRUCTURE WHEN THERE IS AMBIGUITY

Sometimes it sounds great to surround yourself with a team of type A players. Wouldn't you jump for that opportunity? You might be running the risk of having too many people trying to be the boss. And when everyone is trying to manage one important project, conflicts may arise. It gets complicated to agree on a direction, and the result is inferior.

Still, you may want to pull together the mental power of many strong team players—if you can do so without creating a state of confusion. How would you manage a chaos of this nature? Is it too complex to employ numerous experts on one project?

A good example to look at is the way things work on *Iron Chef* or a similar TV show. There is only one head chef, and he is the one in charge of the menu creation, the use of resources (ingredients and people), and the final design. The head chef may have one sous chef and a few station chefs.

So when you have a big project "to cook," only one person—your project manager—should make the final decisions in planning, directing, and execution. The second-in-command, the direct assistant, will be responsible for scheduling and coordinating the operation. Sometimes, the project is not so big and could be managed without an assistant.

Running a huge project is not a daily occurrence. Then again, you'd be surprised how many times you could find yourself in the middle of an "almost chaos" full of experts trying to call the shots. When you are surrounded by type A personalities, keep in mind that top performers like to be responsible for an outcome. Create a responsibility structure as quickly as possible, using the following steps:

1. Declare who the executive chef is and, if needed, who the sous chef is.
2. Evaluate your project. Define the stations or areas of expertise. In each area, have one station chef—your area manager, in case you have more than one person contributing in this area, or your area expert.
3. Communicate the structure and the responsibilities to everybody.
4. Enjoy cooking!

Who is the executive chef on your most complex current project?

Session 42

LET OTHERS STEP UP AND STEP IN

Have you ever taken on a few tasks that someone else on your team was supposed to do? Apparently, that is common in any workplace. The work has to get done, whether the employee is there or not. Occasionally, a knee-jerk reaction of the manager is to personally do the work. Managers are the last line of defense and naturally feel they must hold the fort.

As a manager, you may feel the call of duty in the following circumstances:

- Someone is sick.
- Someone made a costly mistake.
- Someone just left and the position is not filled yet.
- Someone is still not well-versed in the complexity of a task.
- An important presentation is coming up, and you'd like to ensure the results are impeccable.

So *should* you fill in? Not necessarily. Your first approach should be to choose another capable team member who can step up to fill the task before you step down to do so. Sometimes, it will be a learning opportunity for that individual. In some cases, you may want to be somewhat more involved. Have a team member take care of the small details while you meet with that individual frequently to communicate expectations clearly and act as adviser.

Get your own hands dirty only as a last resort, because that comes with a price. When you personally do a detailed task that someone else at a much lower pay scale should have done, you not only waste resources but you also divert your focus from your real responsibility: leading your business unit.

Whenever the need for an emergency takeover arises, ensure that this is not becoming one of your regular tasks by

- deciding on the criteria to shift the job back to its rightful owner and
- communicating the transitional nature of your involvement.

Which task really doesn't "belong" to you?

Session 43

UNDERSTAND THE LONG-TERM IMPACT OF YOUR PRAISE

Recently, I was caught speechless twice. And that doesn't happen very often.

It happened when I received messages from employees with whom I worked over ten years ago. It's not like they popped up out of nowhere. We did stay in touch during those years—but, I have to admit, in a very loose fashion. I'll share with you some of their words:

- "You've always been so giving to me in so many ways."
- "I won't forget your faith in my abilities."
- "You were supportive when it really counted."

Each of them had contacted me to share some news. And if you think that they wanted to get something in return, that assumption has no hold. None of these communications had to do with them asking a thing of me—or me asking them for testimonials. While I sincerely believe that a good word goes a long way, I never imagined that anyone would remember such things a decade later. I was pleasantly surprised and, yes, left speechless by these kind words.

Their remembrances sealed one of the foundations of my teaching: praise makes a difference. A huge one! I encourage my clients to use positive feedback as an effective way to engage and motivate employees. You'll be amazed by the change it creates in your organization.

Effective praise means you discuss the way the task was done, the skills and the attitude used to make it happen, and the impact it had on some high-level goals, if applicable. You thank people for their efforts (and perhaps their initiative) that contributed to the result. Note that some employees do not feel comfortable with praise in front of a team, but that only means you'll make sure you deliver praise one-on-one.

You think that motivating people only comes naturally to leaders?

Well, you know what? Each one of us is a leader. That includes *you*. So when you have something positive to say to your employees about a task they've accomplished, say it.

Who will you give praise to this week?

Session 44

DEFINE "DO YOUR BEST"

Do you recall the last time you asked your team to do their best? Or maybe you were asked to give your best so a complex project could be accomplished in a timely manner? Some managers expect their employees to put in more time and late hours, explaining that tough times call for tough measures. What would you do?

If you consider that crunch time possibly gets people focused, you can probably achieve an immediate increase in performance and prompt results. However, as a long-term strategy, demanding long hours every day is a surefire way to exhaust your team.

A while ago, I was assigned an urgent and critical project. The team in place was known for putting in enormous amounts of overtime, and yet they missed each and every milestone. With a clear understanding that they were all burnt out, I decided to use a different tactic.

I required their best while at work. It was no longer about the amount of time they clocked in—overtime was simply not allowed. Instead, we minimized distractions in the office. I inspired them to spend time with their families and loved ones at the end of each normal workday. It was important that they recharge and reconnect with what was really important in their lives. The plain result was a significant increase in focus and productivity within weeks.

As a leader, once you give your team a meaningful perspective, you want to help individuals make a transition to start operating at a higher level of productivity by encouraging them to stay focused while they are at the office. Frequent status reviews with your team and with individuals will help them see that they can produce and show results while also "having a life."

What is a significant value that could connect your team with their purpose?

Session 45

INSPIRE SELF-STARTERS

From time to time, we expect the people who work for us or with us to show some initiative. And when they don't, we become a little disappointed. Sound familiar?

Just as we aim to give feedback, we may find it awkward to explain what the problem is. How come?

Expecting initiative is an oxymoron. If you expect a certain behavior or action, wouldn't you say what you need accomplished? Once you have defined what you expect, where is the opportunity for taking initiative? On the other hand, when you wait and wait for initiative that never materializes and finally display your frustration, a common response is, "Why didn't you say so?"

Calling out lack of initiative is confusing to both sides. And yet managers often rate their employees based on aptitude toward initiatives.

To clarify where initiative could be expected, let's revisit some assumptions about initiative. How true is it that someone who doesn't initiate has inferior productivity? Or is too lazy? Some employees work well with clear instructions. Others need a general idea of the required result and can figure out how to get things done on their own.

Having a capacity to initiate requires a person to be able to think freely, come up with ideas, and be willing to take some risks. Initiative carries no guarantee of success, and so initiative will be impossible if the environment has no tolerance for mistakes and new ideas are not encouraged.

As a leader, consider the area in your business where you are willing to explore some new ideas. That will be a perfect area for employees to experience taking low-risk initiative. Make it known that you are looking for self-starters in that scope of work and only then see who is ready to take initiative.

When, finally, someone undertakes a project on his or her own initiative, choose carefully how you critique that person's work, if you have to. Be sure to praise that brave individual for trying and use this experience as a teaching tool.

Where would you like your employees to take initiative?

Session 46

DO YOUR EMPLOYEES KNOW YOU CARE?

When I speak to employees about their managers, I sometimes hear a phrase like, "He is only interested in himself." Employees who feel that no one takes care of them display low engagement. The result is not only devastating to the growth of any business but it also brings levels of unnecessary stress to both the team and the manager. What can be done?

Learning from top CEOs reveals that they take specific actions to maintain a clear communication line with employees through roundtables and field visits. Some CEOs encourage all their managers to follow suit. A simple action that a manager can take on a frequent basis is to ask employees, "How can I help you?"

Note that this question doesn't mean that you, as a manager, are taking on the responsibility for their tasks. Your aim is to identify any resources or training that could help employees do their job better. Possibly you can identify barriers that you can help remove. In the process, you make it clear that you care about your employees. That alone will motivate employees to care about your company.

One of the most important tasks of a leader is to build employee confidence. If employees feel that they clearly know what they are supposed to do, they are up for the task. When they know that their contribution is valued, they are motivated to do the best they can.

**What action will you take this coming week
to show your employees that you care?**

PART 4

GROW YOURSELF

When something doesn't go as planned, it's easy to point a finger at someone else. However, as you read through this book, you will see one thread running through each and every segment: *you*. To grow your business, you need to grow yourself. If you expect to see a real change in your business, you need to look within yourself for what needs to change. What worked for you in the past has allowed you to accomplish your successes so far. It has also stopped you from advancing your agenda.

The hardest stone to turn is coming up. It is time to identify your weaknesses, acknowledge your strengths, and transform ... you.

Session 47

MAKE A COMMITMENT

Do you recall the last game when your favorite sport team won? Whether you are a basketball, football, or hockey enthusiastic, the principles behind winning are the same. When each player puts in 100 percent effort during the game, the chance of winning increases.

A serious player is defined by how much he is committed to his sport, and as a result, he is picked to play for his team. Similarly, a runner in a professional race crosses the finish line with an outstanding time after numerous hours of training.

The truth is that every professional athlete can reach these kinds of results only because of their commitment. That commitment is translated into taking daily actions consistently. Without such a commitment, extraordinary results are impossible.

Are you committed to your game? To be in the game—your business branding, your leadership in your industry, your market share—you need to be in the game consistently. To be a professional player in your field, you must engage yourself and practice daily.

What is the game you want to win in your profession?

Session 48

GIVE 100 PERCENT AND THEN SOME

To many of us, 100 percent represents perfection, the ideal, and a real accomplishment. As you strive to achieve perfection in any area of your business and life, there are always challenges.

Sometimes your ideal looks so grand, so far, and so out of reach. To some individuals, that may be demotivating. Even after making a true effort—making calls to prospects on your list, overcoming a long backlog, starting to lay out a new organizational structure, or any other major challenge—you get a sense that you haven't moved the needle much.

Two elements are required for achieving a perfect state: being open-minded and being dedicated. By constantly trying to improve what you do and how you do it, you'll become more efficient, and the effort you invest will bring better and better results. As you move the needle a little at a time, consider each advance an accomplishment.

In essence, the key to perfection is improving yourself. Each week, when you put another idea into action, you take another small step toward excellence leadership.

**What action are you prepared to take
this week to improve your game?**

Session 49

KICK THE WISHY-WASHY DEADLINE HABIT FOR GOOD

Dread. Frustration. Disappointment.

These are just a few of the feelings that come up when you procrastinate. The result is that things that need to get done to further your business stay on the back burner. Do you avoid setting deadlines? Let's get to the root of the problem of dealing with procrastination and project completion. It all begins with setting deadlines efficiently. When setting deadlines is dismissed as unimportant, the ineffectiveness only begins.

In order for a deadline to be effective, there must be a specific task or project to complete and a definite time to complete it by. If there's no specific task and no specific time, there's no deadline.

Deadlines are the foundation of every project. You can't build a house without coordinating the deadlines of all parties involved. Setting those expectations and making them known enables the parties to allocate resources efficiently. This principle applies to any project where people work together and need to be counted on to produce tangible results. Deadlines are just the vehicle that makes the coordination work.

And yet many people avoid setting deadlines because deadlines can bring anxiety, stress, and tension to any interaction. With that in mind, think of how much tension and stress will follow if your project is not being completed because the work of your team is not coordinated.

Overcoming deadline dismissal is not easy. It involves setting an accountability structure that includes drawing a line in the sand (mentally) and placing value on your word. The best accountability structure is the one that is based on sharing your intentions with others, preferably with someone who will not be afraid to call you on it (that includes your employees, in most cases).

Which of your projects is in current need of specific deadlines?

Session 50

IDENTIFY HABITS THAT NO LONGER SERVE YOU

Businesspeople tend to be deliberate about work results. Therefore, when it becomes apparent that routines, habits, or even second-nature actions are obstacles to accomplishments, this should fuel the choice to change. However, becoming aware of those habits that need replacement is not so easy.

Usually, individuals make New Year's resolutions like changing a diet, drinking more water, starting to exercise, or finally seeing a doctor. Why not get some additional energy from the official start of the year and kiss some old habits good-bye? Note that making a resolution that relates to your own habits at work is not setting a business goal. The best time to complete that task is in the later months of the prior year.

If you want to direct some pizzazz from New Year's toward a more successful career, ask yourself the following questions:

- Do I have a work habit that is not propelling me toward my goals?
- What could I do instead?
- What would be the result of sticking to my new habit?
- What am I losing if I give up that old habit?

If you are ready to let go of the old habit and assume a new one, tell someone who'll support you and keep you accountable.

What habit you are willing to replace?

Session 51

SHARE THE LOAD

Over the past two weeks, my health has taken a bad turn. Or maybe the real turn happened a few days prior to that. I started to note little changes in my physical energy. Although I was aware that I was not at full strength, I continued my normal juggling from dawn until late at night: coaching, teaching, supporting my kids in their activities (which is a job on its own), supporting anything necessary in our home, and doing some volunteering. And I continued putting 100 percent into everything I did.

I was getting worse and I felt it. But I was thinking to myself, *I'm strong. I can do it!* It didn't even occur to me that it was time to ask someone for help—someone like a friend. The voice in my head insisted, "You can take care of it by yourself! Why do you need anybody else to help?" So I kept going for a few more days until I was *down!* High fever, shivers, and constant pain, with complications that are still being addressed as I write these lines.

I couldn't even get myself to see the doctor. Yet life around me still needed to be juggled. My younger daughter still needed rides here to there, but I was fired as a chauffeur because I had lost my mobility. I started to connect with my friends. That's what friends are for. It came to me loud and clear that they were there for me as they took upon themselves the tasks that I was finally willing to let go of. This kept going for a few days. The juggling game of my life continued with my friends' gracious assistance. The only ball that dropped was me. This left me all the time I needed to reflect.

I could have listened to my initial symptoms, asked for a little help, and taken care of my own medical needs while everything continued at its normal rhythm. What stopped me was my own limiting belief.

How many times have you told yourself, "Why do I need to ask for help? I can do it myself!"? This thought can permeate every aspect of your life: business and personal. It changes your expectations, your communication, and your results. Next time you hear this inner voice, ask yourself the following:

- What would be the cost of doing it all by myself?
- What can be gained if I engage others in sharing this load?

Where could you use some help?
Can you share your load?

Session 52

IDENTIFY THE QUALITIES OF A HERO

A few days ago, one of my friends acknowledged with heartfelt sympathy the death of one of my military leaders: Ariel Sharon. Sharon was considered the greatest field commander in Israel's history and one of the country's greatest military strategists. I remember hearing the news media covering his ideas, his speeches, and his actions so often as I grew up. A man of accomplishments he was, and certainly a controversial figure. No doubt his legacy will be discussed for many years to come.

There are many people who, like Sharon, make their mark on our world. Some of them may be our own personal heroes. Did you admire a hero when you were growing up? What specifically made you admire that person or that leader?

Here are just a few common traits of leaders:

- inspiring
- excellent at public speaking
- confident
- passionate
- compassionate
- skilled at analytical problem solving

Take a moment and think about a person you hold in high regard and outline three traits that impressed you the most.

Would it be worthwhile for you to develop heroic qualities within yourself?

Session 53

HOW CAN YOU IMPROVE YOUR CRISIS-MANAGEMENT SKILLS?

Has life presented you with stressful situations where you suddenly had new and critical information that you needed to act on immediately? In an instant, your thoughts can get clouded, and your confidence in being able to resolve a crisis can be diminished. All of a sudden, quick thinking is no longer in your reach.

This was the case when I was last traveling abroad and realized my daughter's passport had expired. I will save you the mundane details but pass on the lesson I learned. I have to admit I lost quite a few heartbeats, as I was fully aware that the responsibility was mine and no one else's. There was no one to blame but me—and if there was, would it make any difference?

The fact that I did not look to blame anyone else allowed me to focus right away on only one thing: resolving the situation. First, I inquired about my options.

The solution that was initially presented seemed the only viable one. Sure, it was easier for everyone involved—mainly the authorities. But it was almost impossible for me to carry out, as I was on my way to give a seminar in another part of the country, and the clock was literally ticking before the beginning of a long weekend when all government offices would be closed for business. So I kept pressing and asked: What else is possible? What else can I do to accommodate the situation? And when I did, I got something to work with. I found an alternative that worked for all parties as long as I accessed additional specific resources. My mind cleared, and I started to line up those resources.

When you perceive a situation to be a crisis, it becomes emotional, and it's hard to make decisions. It's debilitating. Many people try to find out whose fault it is. Although it may be relevant for a later lesson learned, at the time of the crisis consider whether you truly want to get caught looking for a culprit. Will doing so promote a quick end result? In order to manage a crisis, your best approach is to dismiss the thought that it is a crisis.

That doesn't mean it's not a challenging situation. But leave the drama for later. Here are some tips for moving forward when it seems like you are going through a critical situation:

- Do not waste precious time figuring out who to blame.
- Start asking questions that focus on resolution.
- Get the facts.
- Identify possibilities.
- Communicate with those who can help you.
- Get in action.

How can your current crisis be corrected?

Session 54

KNOW THYSELF

All human beings have two distinctive personalities—idealistic and pragmatic. As we grow up, many of us depart from the idealistic within us and become pragmatic in every aspect of our lives. And here is how it could end up:

- If we develop a career, we accept job conditions as they are—the office, the commute, the nine-to-five schedule.
- If we start a business, we become consumed by what needs to be done, even to the point of forgetting what it was like when we were dreaming about how far we could take our business idea.

When you're being pragmatic, you take the situation for granted and stop asking an important question: Why should things be the way they are? You regard your decisions as sensible and mature, as expected of an adult, and at the same time you often act as if on autopilot. You risk becoming hardheaded just because you are trying to complete your checklist. For the record, working with a checklist is not a bad idea. But forgetting the big picture is. Why do you and so many other people focus on to-dos and forget about aspirations?

The idealistic part of you will be at the mercy of the pragmatic part of you unless you decide to give yourself some space to examine opportunities along the way and consider how they fit in the big picture of what you'd really like to achieve. Reviewing the big picture once in a while can reconnect you with your own purpose and energize you to either continue on your venture or change course.

Here are some points to consider when reviewing your big picture:

- What am I good at?
- What do I enjoy doing?
- What brings me satisfaction?
- What else do I want to accomplish in my life?

Look at various aspects not only in the short term, but also in the long term: career development, personal development, relationships, family, financial aspirations, joy, health, and wellness. When was the last time you stimulated your mind with possibilities?

With whom would you choose to explore those possibilities?

Session 55

HOW CAN I MAKE A SOUND DECISION?

Have you ever made a decision while upset and then regretted it later? Making decisions while you are all charged up robs you of sound judgment. Your emotional reaction can prevent you from seeing all sides of a problem and identifying the best solutions.

First, be aware that you are having an emotional reaction. Anger, frustration, confusion, hurt, bewilderment, and sadness are only some of the emotions you can experience. Having these emotions is totally okay. Take a moment to identify what happened. Get the facts and stick to them. Simplify by leaving out your interpretation, analysis, or opinion of those facts.

Still feeling emotional? Delay your decision just a bit to allow yourself time to clear your head. Healthy delays are designed to blow off steam and may include

- confiding in a friend,
- exercising, or
- engaging in other healthy coping mechanisms that work for you.

That way, you can make the decisions that are best for you, your organization, and others around you.

Which decision troubles you these days?

Session 56

DO YOU SET UP YOUR OWN THINK TANK?

Our new economy has made the problems that businesses encounter increasingly complex. The speed is faster, the markets are more volatile, and the stakes are higher. For that reason, you may want to entertain the wisdom and experience of a group of diverse, educated experts. Most small businesses cannot afford think tanks of PhDs trained in various approaches.

Besides relying on gut feelings or the opinions of trusted employees, some business owners ask an ally for an opinion. Although getting another perspective is helpful, it has its own limitations. It gets you only as far as the specifics of prior problems and observations. What if the problem you face has a set of variables that neither you nor your ally have worked with in the past? In that case, you need to create a framework for freely discussing broader solutions: that is, your own think tank, or possibly a mastermind group with other business owners. Your framework should include

- people you trust for their experience and their teamwork approach,
- preset rules of engagement, and
- a facilitator who has nothing to gain from one solution or another.

An effective facilitator ensures you hear all valid solutions. Such individuals are excellent listeners, analytical, and friendly. When multiple business owners cover the expense of a mastermind facilitator, the cost is a fraction of having a think tank on board.

Sometimes you are confronted by a complex problem where the stakes are high, and you think you can solve it using the talent you have in-house. However, when a manager facilitates this important brainstorming, others at the table may hold back their ideas for one reason or another. If that happens, set up your own think tank and look for someone from the outside who is capable of facilitating the search for a unique solution.

What is a challenge you can use to get a group of people to *think together?*

Session 57

MASTER YOUR CRAFT

Masters are few and far between in their industry. It takes time, effort, energy, and money to master your craft. It involves trying new approaches, failing, and being disappointed. It means adjusting, constantly improving, and never settling.

Why bother mastering your profession?

A more intriguing question is "Why not?"

Continued training in your craft enables you to make wiser decisions, influence more people, gain respect, stay ahead of your competition, and be more effective at what you do. It takes courage to fail and dedication to get back up again, time after time.

If you are a professional businessperson, what does mastery look like? What does it mean if you are a professional manager? Mastery becomes more complex if you play more than one role in your job. To break it down to the necessary elements, ask yourself the following:

- What are the core skills I need to master?
- Of those, what is the one key skill that, if improved, would dramatically increase my effectiveness?
- What is one straightforward action I could take to improve that skill?
- What kind of training do I need to become a master?

What kind of mastery you could hold?

Session 58

TAKE A LONGER VIEW

Many business owners put a priority on actions that take care of the bottom line in the immediate future by improving daily operations, generating higher revenues, and increasing return on investment. Who wouldn't want that?

You might have already taken a class or attended a seminar to get up to speed and learn new methods of completing tasks. After all, your incentives may be directly linked to your capacity to push forward projects and do that consistently. Surprisingly, large companies who have taken part in research realize that when their employees do not focus on long-term goals, their ability to sustain high performance over time decreases. In the long run, the company's health is affected.

That phenomenon is not limited to employees in large companies. Small business owners should keep in mind that being mindful of long-term objectives is no less important than always being concerned with immediate results.

If you wish to sustain a consistent level of performance, it's time to review your own long-term personal goals. How about suggesting to your employees that they do so as well—or maybe even arrange for an in-house workshop to help them see the benefit they can gain from doing so?

When do you plan to go over your long-term goals?

Session 59

DO SOMETHING OUTSIDE YOUR COMFORT ZONE

When was the last time you tried a new food? Went skydiving? Sang karaoke? Danced with a partner? It may seem silly, but experiences like these help train your brain to leave your comfort zone. Kids do it all the time as part of their growth process.

How might becoming more comfortable with things outside your comfort zone be valuable in the office? Maybe you're uncomfortable delivering certain communications. Maybe public speaking scares the hell out of you. Maybe you've been afraid to receive feedback. And that translates into becoming stagnant professionally.

The business environment may be the last place you would consider breaking loose. Yet the momentum needed to leave your comfort zone could propel your career growth. Ask yourself: If I could conquer one specific professional fear, what would it be?

Here is some good news: getting used to leaving your comfort zone is a leadership skill that works everywhere. By applying it, you can reap the rewards—not only an interesting and energizing lifestyle but also an ability to take important actions in the office that you would have otherwise avoided.

I, for one, plan on taking a helicopter ride soon to check the limits of my fear of heights.

When does your next adventure begin?

Session 60

KEEP YOUR PERCEPTION POSITIVE

Some mornings you start your day without the energy to lead your business or even yourself. You follow your task list or go through your appointment schedule, but you feel unable to generate any excitement within yourself, and anything you accomplish is purely by inertia. You'd play hooky that day if you could, since you're pretty sure you won't be able to advance any opportunity that crosses your path anyway. Sound familiar?

Yet some people seem to exude positive energy on a regular basis. Where can you fill up with that? By meeting with people who motivate you? Listening to music or words of encouragement? Although these are valid methods, it's important to understand that ultimately, positive energy comes from within.

Really? Can you control whether you have positive energy or you don't? The answer may be simple, but it's not easy to implement.

Your energy comes from your perception of life. Since the perception is yours, you definitely have control over it. When you are intentional about being positive, no matter what, you experience different kinds of interactions with people around you, leading to remarkable results. So being intentional is what allows some people to emanate passion, excitement, and enthusiasm consistently.

To start tapping into your inner positive energy pool, start the day by asking yourself what will be your intention for today. And as you take your midday break, ask yourself how that intention is coming into play.

What can you do right now to adjust your perception?

Session 61

WHO CAN HELP YOU NEXT?

Many business owners I have coached share a similar concern: "It's lonely at the top." If you share that belief, I bet it makes you feel burdened by the responsibility. How stressed are you about having to steer your ship on your own?

The good news is that you can ease that load by identifying the people who are best suited to help you achieve your most important goals. Are they mentors? Colleagues? Coaches? Advisers? Professionals in another field? Each goal may demand a different individual, but here's the point: there are people out there willing and able to open just the right doors for you. You are not alone. All you need to figure out is who and what to ask.

Who could you call in to boost your progress today?

Session 62

WHAT IS DRIVING YOU?

Sometimes, amidst your midday tasks, you may feel your energy level drop. That's quite normal. What you do to overcome this sudden fatigue depends on your past experiences.

You may talk to others, meditate, eat a snack, drink coffee, or stretch just so you can focus on the next item on your to-do list. And it works, except that these are just outside stimulants to get you going. Have you ever wondered where you got your initial energy to build your business or career?

Why is that important? Because connecting with that internal source is the key to keeping yourself in the game, rain or shine, and improving your game when you want to.

If any of the following is something you are interested in, you'd better get to know who you are at your core:

- expanding your businesses
- advancing your career
- creating a legacy

Spend some time rediscovering the powerful feeling that compels you to do the most difficult tasks. In other words, what are you passionate about when it comes to your occupation?

When you find a way to harness your passion into a specific area of your business, you'll have the resilience required to make your business successful. When you combine that with a lively interest in what is being accomplished, you acquire a powerful inner duo: passion and enthusiasm.

Next time you connect to your inner drive, make the impossible possible. Use your passion and enthusiasm to conquer the challenges that were keeping you back.

What makes you tick?

Session 63

WHEN DO YOU STOP LEARNING?

Many high school seniors and students apply for scholarships these days as they plan to continue their studies at college. With luck, this task will pay off. Needless to say, their investment in their future isn't small change. Obviously, they and their parents place a high value on education. Otherwise, they wouldn't bother.

No matter when you had your last educational experience, you learned lessons that somehow are wired to how you do things today. Your studying experience might have built your technical ability, increased your knowledge bank, or even improved your interpersonal skills. Although formal training is not necessary for conscious learning, one has to be open to looking at things from a different point of view and welcome his or her own growth.

When someone tells me, "You can't teach an old dog new tricks," I respond, "And what does that get you?" If you understand that you can still learn new things that would be useful to your growth, you don't need to apply for a scholarship. You just need to ask yourself the following:

- What am I open to learn that will sharpen my game?
- What skills are important to improve even after my formal education program is over?
- Is there any training that could help me develop the skills that are needed for my success?

How open are you to continuing to learn?

Session 64

MAKE AN ANY-TIME-OF-YEAR'S RESOLUTION

Some say that making a New Year's resolution on New Year's Day starts your year with the right focus. So what if you were too busy celebrating to take a moment and think of what you wanted to accomplish this year? And now you are getting back into your everyday routine. Have you missed your window of opportunity? You may have lost the excitement of the moment, but you can open a new window of opportunity to accomplish something that was a challenge until now.

Some people avoid making a resolution, saying it's just like making any other decision. What makes a decision you make a "resolution" that could stick? The following are important:

- firmness of purpose
- a formal way of expressing your intention

The bottom line is that you have not lost the opportunity to become focused on a huge undertaking, even if it seems that the clock has already moved forward. To move ahead, get clear on what you want to accomplish and express it to others.

What is a worthwhile objective for this year?

Session 65

KISS DOUBT GOOD-BYE

Have you ever had anyone impede your plans just by raising doubt about your actions, intentions, or dreams? If today is like any other day, you're more than likely rushing through life, doing your best to stay focused on your objectives and get things done despite obstacles, some of which you are not even aware of.

Whether your plan involves business or is of a personal nature, suddenly an obstacle is introduced.

The worst enemy of your progress at this point is your own negative thinking that you might not be able to overcome that obstacle. Mr. Doubt creeps in. Remember him?

It is natural to have another voice in your head. It's part of being human. Wait a second—that means there is a first voice there too. You know, the one that encourages you to proceed no matter what. It is known as positive thinking. When we develop that voice, we tend to listen less to Mr. Doubt. The problem is that we hardly ever exercise our inner thinking.

But today is not just another day. Today, you are going to start exercising your positive thinking with five simple actions. Every day for the next twenty-one days, do the following:

1. Write down three *new* things you are grateful for.
2. Exercise just a bit more than you used to before, because you can.
3. Perform one random act of kindness, and watch the impact you have.
4. Take a short break (shut your eyes and concentrate on your breathing).

5. Add three extra smiles to your day, and see the responses you get.

How cool would it be if a friend or a colleague joined you too? There would be less negative thinking around you.

How open are you to discovering what you are grateful for?

Session 66

ARE YOU HANDLING THE PERFECT WORKLOAD?

Some people can handle various tasks in tandem and are referred to as master multitaskers. It seems that they don't miss a beat. Or so you think.

The ability to multitask used to be considered such an advantage that a few years ago my multitasking skills were rated on the annual performance review as if they were a badge of honor in the environment of corporate America. However, research by business professor Sophie Leroy at Minnesota University in 2009 has shown that when people keep switching between tasks, they lose time and become less productive. Evidently time is needed to refocus on the task at hand and overcome what Leroy calls *attention residue* from what your mind was dealing with a second ago.

Are you a heavy multitasker? Imagine how much time you lose if you handle complex tasks and toggle them on and off. If you strive to work productively, ask yourself the following questions:

- What is the maximum load of tasks that I can handle simultaneously without starting to forget key points?
- Do I find myself working better when I focus on one item at a time?
- What are some situations that involve considerations like safety that require me to completely avoid distractions?

Increasing your awareness is the first step in making timely choices about responding (or not responding) to distractions.

How would your daily routine change if you could handle the workload differently?

Session 67

DOES ADMINISTRATIVE WORK GET IN YOUR WAY?

Earlier this week, I presented in a business expo. Knowing that I would be meeting many business owners and managers like you, I took the opportunity to compile a survey.

The number-one time waster, according to my participants, was administrative work. Now, if that is what you were hired to do, then it *is* your real work. And if you still call it a time waster, it's time to change your attitude or your career. However, if your real craft is something different, you may find administrative work frustrating. Yet it has to be done.

When does it become a time drain? When you do not feel that you can control how much time is spent doing that activity. That's when you avoid engaging in it until you absolutely have to. By this point, you are already tired and distracted (thinking about being somewhere else doing some fun stuff), and as a result, your focus is not really there, increasing the risk of making mistakes. The bottom line is that it takes you more time, and most importantly, it drains your energy.

Now, most of us just want to do what we are good at, so we get the results that we want. Where is the choice? You may want to ask yourself the following questions:

- In order to get the level of results I aspire for, how much administrative work do I need to do?
- What amount of time does it make sense to allocate to administrative work?
- Do I have support staff to help me in getting this work squared away?
- What would be left for me to do to ensure the quality of results?

When you start making choices about your administrative work, you start wrapping your hands around managing your own time, and you become more positive about the chances of having time left to do some fun and meaningful stuff. When you manage your time, you start feeling in control, and your energy level rises.

Take a moment. Think about how much time you spent this last week on administrative work. Before next week starts, take up a challenge of planning your week based on the questions above.

What will you do to get that administrative work out of your negative thoughts?

Session 68

WHAT IS YOUR RESPONSE TIME?

Remember that e-mail to an associate of yours a week ago requesting a particular action? And you haven't heard back yet? You might be tempted to make the following excuses on that individual's behalf:

- "She might have missed my e-mail."
- "He must be really busy and has a lot on his plate."
- "She may need to research some options before she gets back to me."
- "He will probably get back to me the minute he gets a chance to read it."

And maybe it is just as simple as that. Of course, if this has happened a few times before, your thoughts will be more like the following:

- "Wow. I wonder if she doesn't read my e-mails."
- "Maybe he is not the right person for these kinds of issues."
- "I guess she has other things that are more important than getting back to me."
- "Maybe I shouldn't count on him anymore."

You see, the fact that someone is busy doesn't change a bit the perception the lack of a timely response creates. What does that mean to you and your own responsiveness? You need to keep in mind that whether your relationships are business-related or not, you are responsible for the timeliness of your responses.

The fast pace of our integrated digital world creates higher expectations for timeliness. Needless to say, in the business world, you may miss opportunities when you don't act in a timely manner.

You may want to define a specific time slot each day for handling your e-mail responses. Clarify for others your expectations on response time as well. In fact, you may want to create a footer on your automatic e-mail reply for business that states what the expected response time is.

What do you consider an appropriate time to respond by e-mail to your associates?

Session 69

DISMANTLE YOUR ASSUMPTIONS

When was the last time you looked at what you take for granted? Oftentimes, we assume that what worked a certain way in the past will continue to work the same way. When it comes to the operation of your business, it's important to recognize that things do change. Consider the following thoughts:

- My hard-working employees will continue to take on extra assignments.
- My vendors are unwilling to renegotiate pricing.
- My customers are willing to tolerate delays.

How true are any of these? Experiencing something in the past doesn't mean the same thing will happen in the future, and it can create a blind spot. Sometimes, having assumptions like the above will stop you from pursuing opportunities or resolving issues before they become dramas or disasters waiting to happen.

What are some of the assumptions you're making right now that may limit your organization's performance either now or in the future?

Session 70

DON'T LET UNSUPPORTIVE PEOPLE GET YOU DOWN

In a perfect world, the people who surround you support you, encourage you, and at times even cheer you on. But who lives in a perfect world? Let's first understand what supporting really means to a leader, a manager, or a business owner like yourself. Do you expect your colleagues, your team, and perhaps your friends and family to stand behind every idea you come up with? To encourage you relentlessly no matter what? Or even to charge ahead and help you implement your vision?

Quite honestly, only some people in your life may take that route, and only to some extent. To put things in perspective, a natural approach for people is to question you. And yet questioning doesn't mean that they don't support you. Some questioning is relevant and helpful because it allows you to have a 360-degree view of how your ideas could make a difference. Here are some supportive angles for questioning:

- clarifying a meaning
- examining how things will get done
- verifying your goals

On the other hand, it is important to also be aware of the kind of questions that are not supportive. These are questions that do the following:

- instill doubt in your capabilities
- interject fear of any kind
- bring up limiting beliefs

Those nonsupportive questions would, at best, have you think things through again. At worst, the impact could be devastating. Be aware that this could trigger a vulnerable state of mind in which you can't count on yourself to generate the results you are aiming for.

Review how you normally respond to those unsupportive individuals. It is not easy to stop them from doing what they are used to doing. However, you can say something like, "I get what you are trying to say, but I have my view (or my experience) to count on."

Who is triggering your doubt or fear?

Session 71

KNOW YOUR WEAKNESSES AND YOUR STRENGTHS

For years now, I have been working with individuals who seek to up their game, and I've seen the results they achieve through improvement. I have found that even across industries and all different sizes of companies, an internal personal dilemma is quite consistent. When you engage in discovering your own leadership style, you may learn that you share more than you think with these successful leaders.

Frequently, improvement starts with looking at the actions you have taken and those actions that you need to take but for some mysterious reason haven't. Ultimately, the real gain becomes clear when you look inside at who you really are. Sensitive leaders tend to pick apart their own weaknesses and hardly acknowledge their own strengths. Others harp on their strengths and ignore their weaknesses.

Why does recognizing both your strengths and your weaknesses matter? When you focus mostly on your shortcomings, you develop a feeling of inadequacy. As a result, it becomes harder to initiate projects or face challenges. Can you imagine a sports coach stressing out his team just before they get on the field to play against a tough opponent? For the same reason, when you face any challenge (yes, *any* challenge), the last thing you should focus on is your weaknesses. This will be the time to focus on your strengths and plan how you can leverage them.

With that being said, when would be a good time to note your weaknesses?

A while ago, I read an article regarding the second-in-command in army units. It was evident that successful generals look to select individuals who are very different from them to be their "number two" in order to bring something additional to the command team.

Knowing your weaknesses allows you to pursue individuals with complementary skills to strengthen your team in those areas in which you cannot bring your best. Before recruiting, make sure you identify your weaknesses.

This week, take some time to uncover your own strengths and weaknesses.

What are your three most valuable strengths as well as three of your weaknesses?

Session 72

FEEL LIKE A WINNER

There are days when you've just closed a great deal, you had a fascinating presentation, you came up with a new innovative solution, or you just completed an amazing race, and you feel like you are on top of the world. You may think, *That was a job well done*, or *I was able to make a difference today*. The experience of winning affects your approach to all your undertakings. It affects how you interact with people in your business and in your personal life. It affects your level of focus and productivity.

In essence, it is like adding high-octane fuel to your engine. It is helpful to understand what triggers that feeling. There are two types of references to sensing one's success: external or internal. Let's figure out which one is yours.

Do you believe you did a good job only when others express that to you? Do you rely only on hard numbers (orders, sales, revenue) to convince you that you've made progress? If the above sounds right, you depend on others' words and actions to feel fulfilled.

On the other hand, if you don't need an external reference, you trust your internal feelings, voices, and images as evidence of a personal win. In that case, feeling victorious is independent of external people and events.

Leadership positions require individuals who don't rely on others to tell them they made a good decision. Can you imagine a senior manager who would depend on his staff to tell him he is doing okay?

So, what if you are used to external references and recognition to enjoy success, accomplishment, and fulfillment? Does it mean you cannot be a leader? Does it mean you cannot energize yourself without others' input? Those would be incorrect assumptions. You can develop your own references, internal voices, and belief in yourself so you can reap the rewards of feeling like a winner at your own discretion and start taking on projects of magnitude with vigor. You can read books and listen to motivational audios that will help you to think differently about yourself. For many individuals, working with a coach can speed up that internal growth.

What is one thing you accomplished over the past week that warrants a pat on the back?

Session 73

ARE YOU DOING YOUR BEST?

Whenever you want to improve your professional results in a specific business area, asking yourself "Am I doing my best?" and answering honestly allows you to discover what you are missing. This is a necessary question if you want to excel in both your professional and personal life.

When my clients are seeking to raise the bar, they ask themselves that question. But is that the right question to ask?

Interestingly enough, this question alone is not sufficient for becoming a successful professional. If you are looking to distinguish your business in the marketplace, the necessary question would be, "How can I be the best in what I do so others refer to me as the expert?" That is the door to achieving a whole other level of performance. To find the answer to that question, do the following this week:

- Thoroughly review your skills, experience, service, and accomplishments.
- Identify what is it that makes you shine.
- Make sure to convey that to others.
- Create a support system around you that will keep you true to your intentions whenever the road gets tough.

How can you be the best in what you do?

ENDORSEMENTS

"Tmima gets right to the heart of what truly matters in growing your business."
> —Bruce D. Schneider, founder, iPEC Coaching, author of *Energy Leadership*

"I don't think there could be a better title for this book. From the first paragraph of the first chapter I found I was in a constant mode of professional self-assessment. As a CEO and president of a company, I have to answer to customers' and employees' needs. They are my 'boss.' It is not always easy to get objective feedback. While reading *The Truth*, I found some fresh objectivity and also found myself making a mental list of changes I need to implement in the management of me."
> —Brendan Phillips, president, Smart Carpet and Flooring

"Whether you are a sole practitioner, multilocation operator, or a manager in a large organization, the insights and strategies presented in this book help you reset your sails and point your business in the right direction. Tmima has captured a way to clearly get you to focus on your business, instead of just working in your business and to identify goals to get you to the next level. This book is a must-read for you and those you manage."
> —Michael Ginsberg, executive director and owner of multiple LearningRx Brain Training Centers

"Tmima is a master at leading you through the challenging process of staying focused on your goals while removing barriers to success. Her understanding of how mindfulness intersects with strategy creates a powerful force for your business."
> —Laura Novak Meyer, founder and CEO, Little Nest Portraits

"If I have learned anything in my twenty five plus years of business it is that my success is only limited by the quality of my own thoughts and beliefs. Tmima's work has helped me to identify self-imposed limitations and truly breakthrough to higher levels of success and happiness. I wholeheartedly endorse Tmima's work to anyone who is serious about improving their business and their life!"

-Bryan Klein, CEO and Founder, The MAX Challenge

Open Book Editions
A Berrett-Koehler Partner

Open Book Editions is a joint venture between Berrett-Koehler Publishers and Author Solutions, the market leader in self-publishing. There are many more aspiring authors who share Berrett-Koehler's mission than we can sustainably publish. To serve these authors, Open Book Editions offers a comprehensive self-publishing opportunity.

A Shared Mission

Open Book Editions welcomes authors who share the Berrett-Koehler mission—Creating a World That Works for All. We believe that to truly create a better world, action is needed at all levels—individual, organizational, and societal. At the individual level, our publications help people align their lives with their values and with their aspirations for a better world. At the organizational level, we promote progressive leadership and management practices, socially responsible approaches to business, and humane and effective organizations. At the societal level, we publish content that advances social and economic justice, shared prosperity, sustainability, and new solutions to national and global issues.

Open Book Editions represents a new way to further the BK mission and expand our community. We look forward to helping more authors challenge conventional thinking, introduce new ideas, and foster positive change.

For more information, see the Open Book Editions website:
http://www.iuniverse.com/Packages/OpenBookEditions.aspx

Join the BK Community! See exclusive author videos, join discussion groups, find out about upcoming events, read author blogs, and much more! http://bkcommunity.com/

Printed in the United States
By Bookmasters